MW00473997

BODY LANGUAGE
A quick reference for character action and description

ANN EVERETT

Copyright 2015 by Ann Everett
All right reserved

First print edition, May 2015
ISBN-13:978-1512139464
ISBN-10:1512139467

No part of this publication may be reproduced or
distributed in print or electronic form without prior
permission of the author.

Please respect the hard work of the author and do not
participate in or encourage the piracy of copyrighted
materials.

Book Cover design by: Ann Everett Stock
photo purchased by Ann Everett from
© Ilyaka | Dreamstime.com

ABOUT THE AUTHOR

Award winning author, Ann Everett writes mysteries, new adult romance, and contemporary romance with a dose of Texas twang and Southern sass. She lives in Northeast Texas, where she writes, bakes, and fights her addiction to Diet Dr. Peppers.

Five things Ann's bio doesn't mention:

♥She's been married to the same man since dirt.
♥She loves shopping at thrift stores.
♥She hates talking on the phone.
♥A really sharp pencil makes her happy.
♥She's thankful wrinkles aren't painful.

You can contact Ann at **ann.everett@rocketmail.com**
♥♥**She loves hearing from readers.**

You can visit her site at http://www.anneverett.com

 Stalk her at:

http://www.twitter.com/TalkinTwang

http://www.linkedin.com/pub/ann-everett/38/482/968

http://www.Plus.google.com/108564049431137119227

http://www.pinterest.com/loacl/

https://www.facebook.com/LOACL

TABLE OF CONTENTS

INTRODUCTION
Action (noun)

Something done usually as opposed to something said.
(Princeton's Wordnet)

Something done so as to accomplish a purpose.
(Wiktionary)

Description (noun)

A statement that represents something in words.
(Princeton's Wordnet)

A set of characteristics by which someone or something
can be recognized.
(Wiktionary)

Action and description are key elements in any successful novel. By giving your characters both, the reader *feels* the experience. But how much is too much—or too little?

Inside this book, you'll find lists of actions and descriptions for each body part, along with lots of examples of how to put them together to give your story more punch.

In addition, we'll talk about how to keep the action going, author intrusion, use of adverbs, sentence starts, similes and metaphors.

In place of having categories listed in alphabetical order, I start with body, then work down the torso from the top of the head...hair, head, eyes, etc.

Even though experienced writers may find Body Language useful, it is aimed toward the beginner to intermediate. I hope you find it helpful.

According to U.S. Copyright Circular 34, "Copyright law does not protect names, titles, short phrases or expressions, even if it is novel or distinctive or lends itself to a play on words, it cannot be protected by copyright."

So the sentence starts (short phrases) listed under the **READ TO WRITE** section of this book are freely available for you to use in your writing.

Don't Beat the Reader Over the Head

Overwriting: This is a mistake all new writers make. They over explain either through description or actions.

Here are some examples:

Cowboy Joe pulled his gun belt tight around his waist and buckled it.

See anything wrong with that sentence? Where else do you wear a belt other than your waist? Also, if you change the common verb *pulled* to a stronger one, the reader gets a better picture.

Cowboy Joe cinched his gun belt tight and buckled it.

Here's another one.

"You shot me, you fool!" she screamed, as she pulled a gun from her purse and fired at Joe.

Problem: The exclamation point tells us she's screaming, so the reader doesn't need that tag/attribution, *she screamed.*

Try it this way:

"You shot me, you fool!" She rummaged in her purse, pulled out a gun and returned fire.

One more try with just a bit of description.

"You shot me, you fool!" She rummaged in her purse, produced a small pearl-handled pistol, and returned fire.

Here are some common overwriting mistakes:

She stared up at the ceiling.

Is a ceiling located any other place than up? Same thing with ceiling fan…just stare at it. Don't stare *up* at it.

He sat down on the sofa.

Can you sit on a sofa any other way than down? You can sit up in bed. You can straighten in a chair. You can plop onto a bar stool. Just watch for places you don't need those extra words.

She stood on the balcony and looked down below.

Choose one or the other…*down or below.* They mean the same thing, so only one is needed. Same goes for *up above.*

Here's one with so much description, it over-powers the reason for the sentence.

Jane walked briskly across the high-polished wooden floor of the sunbathed gallery, darting her eyes from painting to painting hung on the bland, white walls as she grabbed her art history book from the upholstered bench where she'd left it the day before.

The problem: The reader doesn't need to know, nor do they care about high-polished wooden floors, upholstered furniture, or bland, white walls. The whole reason for the sentence is to have the character return to the gallery for her book.

Jane returned to the gallery and retrieved the book she'd left there.

Now, if the sunlight or polished floors reminds her of something that pertains to her past and triggers an important thread of the story, then by all means, show the part that causes that. (example below) But don't get so bogged down in writing descriptions just for the sake of description, that you lose the meaning of your story. It's true. Less is more.

Jane's heels clicked across the polished wooden floor of the gallery. Dreams of having her own work displayed on the bland, white walls excited her. *What a silly notion.* Maybe Mom was right. Jane would never be good enough. Moving to the bench, she grabbed her art history book she'd left the day before.

See? If some of that description can be worked into Jane's thoughts about her past or an experience she's had, then it won't sound as just word filler. Because of that little bit, the reader learns Jane and her mom don't have a good relationship and Jane has always fallen short in her mother's eyes.

Stay Out of Your Character's Head

Author intrusion: She/He knew. He/She noticed.

Most of the time when you use these two words to begin a sentence, they can be deleted and the meaning of the sentence doesn't change, and it becomes more active.

Examples:

Maggie knew based on Jace's reputation, he wouldn't be interested.

In Maggie's point of view, everything is being told in her voice. Therefore, it's not necessary to use *Maggie knew.* That's the author telling the reader what Maggie knew! It can be written without those two words and get the same point across. **AND,** the sentence is stronger without it.

Based on Jace's reputation, he wouldn't be interested.

Same thing with noticed…stronger without it. More punch.

He noticed Marc's cocky attitude fade.

Marc's cocky attitude faded.

Sometimes it's a matter of style to use knew and noticed. I doubt readers will stop reading your book if you use them. I even use them sometime, but again, don't overuse them.

I'll also point out something I'm guilty of...one of many things. Above, I wrote...it's not necessary. Has anybody ever told you that when you write *it's not,* it sounds like it's **snot**? Gross! There's a poem about it.

When you're with your honey
And your nose is runny
You may think it's funny
But it's not!

In editing, I try to go through and change those to... it isn't.

KEEP THE ACTION GOING
Passive Voice

Oh, the dreaded passive voice. It's a real killer. Another one of my many problems in writing. I just love the word…was. Again, sometimes, passive voice is necessary to get your point across, and sometimes the sentence sounds better with it, but be careful of using too much. Cut when you can.

http://www.espressoenglish.net has a great definition of passive vs. active.

In the active voice, the subject of the sentence **DOES** the action.

John painted the house last week.

In the passive voice, the subject of the sentence **RECEIVES** the action.

The house was painted last week.

Example of how to fix passive voice using *was*.

His face was twisted with fury.

Take out *was* and voila!

His face twisted with fury.

Example below from **http://www.fiction-doctor.com** another excellent site for writing info.

The boy had gone to the store after he'd gone to school.

Fix by using two verbs.

The boy bicycled to the store after sneaking out of school.

WOULDN'T IT BE LOVELY

Adverbs

Use as few as possible. I recommend not using them at all in dialogue tags.

There should NEVER be a reason to tag dialogue this way: *She screamed angrily.* By the time you get to the character's response to whatever made her angry, the writer should have established that she's mad. If they have, the word *screamed* tells the reader the character is angry, so to describe it is redundant.

I recently ~~read~~ tried to read a book which had an adverb with every dialogue tag. "I couldn't do it!" I said excitedly. I'm not kidding. The author used just about every adverb known to man. She said wistfully. She said softly. She said joyfully. She said happily. She said cheerily. Knowingly. Heartily. Anxiously. Uncertainly. And the list just went on and on.

Tagging with adverbs, in my humble opinion, is lazy writing. Find ways to *show* those emotions so the reader experiences the same thing the character does.

It's much more effective to have heat rise in your character's cheeks, have their voice elevate, back stiffen, face pinch, hands fist. Give the reader those actions and there is no need for *said angrily.*

SIMILES AND METAPHORS

I don't know about you, but I get these two confused. So let's take them one at a time with the definition. All the examples come from **http://www.ereadingworksheets.com** a great site from Mr. Donald Morton. He has lots of teaching info and worksheets on the site, so if you're a school teacher or writer, take a look.

SIMILE is a comparison between two different things using the word **like** or **as** to make the comparison.

The bottle rolled off the table **like** a teardrop.

She hung her head **like** a drying flower.

The children ran **like** ripples through water.

He had hidden his wealth, heaped and hoarded and piled on high **like** sacks of wheat in a granary.

Death is **like** moonlight in a lofty wood that pours pale magic through the shadowy leaves.

Barefooted, ragged, with neglected hair, she was **as** thin **as** a new moon.

Her hair was **as** soft **as** a spider web.

Her laughter was **as** warm **as** a blanket.

The windflowers were **as** yellow striped **as** an adder's tongue.

METAPHOR is a comparison between two **unlike** things not using like or as.

His cotton candy words did not appeal to her taste.

The detective listened to her tales with a wooden face.

John's answer to the problem was just a Band-Aid, not a solution.

She cut him down with her words.

David is a worm for what he did to Phyllis.

We all have shadows on the wall of time.

The promise between us remained a delicate flower.

Similes and metaphors can add a lot to a story, but again, use caution. Sprinkle them in.

READ AND LISTEN TO WRITE

A few bits of advice before we get to the lists and writing examples. To become a better writer, you must read other's work. Especially authors in your genre. Pay attention to how they describe things. How they mix description and action in narrative…and intersperse it with dialogue. Watch how they begin their sentences. Experienced writers don't use a lot of pronouns to start sentences. Take notes and refer back to them when you write.

If you don't belong to a critique group, I highly recommend you join one, either online or one in your area. There are many to choose from online, Critique Circle, FanStory, The Next Big Writer, just to name a few. I belong to thenextbigwriter.com and a local group of writer friends who never pull punches. Once you get accustomed to being critiqued, you won't do without it. It is the most helpful tool I use in writing.

You probably know this, but I'll mention it for those who may be starting out and aren't aware of it. Read your work out loud to yourself. You use a different part of the brain when reading aloud than when reading silently, so you'll pick up on repeat words and awkward sentences.

Once your manuscript is complete, critiqued, and edited, get Beta-readers to read it from start to finish. Writers read differently than readers, so make sure you get at least one reader who doesn't write. That may sound crazy, but readers pick up on things writers don't and vice-versa.

Take a look at the following phrases to begin sentences.

Still babbling with confusion

The question had her blinking
No matter what she wore
Heat ran up her neck
Wary, she looked over her shoulder
Appearing dead serious
Breath strangled in her throat
For one tantalizing moment
Despite his disappointment
More confused by the moment
His inky black hair hung
A half-laugh took her by surprise
Fighting her smile
With a groan, she admitted
In a drunken slur
Under the circumstances
Skeptical at his confession
Light flashed into his peripheral vision
Ignoring her request
But by tomorrow morning
Despite his disappointment
Trying to smooth her skirt
She scowled down at her salad
Turmoil swirling within her
On a soft needy moan
Helpless to stop the emotion
Pushing aside her fear
Unsteady on her feet
Shutting out the voice of reason
Seconds ticked by
To lighten the mood
After a quick prayer
Filled with fear
It took some determination
Fear curled through her stomach
Knuckles cracked,
The audible relief in her tone
Never in her life,

Through her teeth
Regardless of the people around her
For two heartbeats
Holding her breath
Anxiety churned in her stomach
Despite tripping over her own feet
It took some concentration
All humor gone
Too many times
The relief in her tone
With one look
Walking to the wall of windows
Never in her life
Like a fool
Carrying a cup of cocoa
In the blink of an eye
Through her teeth
Giving up
In a handful of years
Comfortable in her pajamas
Long after the last guest departed
Before she could move
In her Monday morning habit
With her TV tuned to channel
A week was long enough
The best way to take our mind off
The first order of business
With a weekend packed with events
Sneaking back into the house
Thanks to her work schedule
In the ballroom
When the room cleared
As the trees thickened
In dealing with her mother
At the stroke of midnight
At five thirty, he came to a dead stop
Beautiful plates the color of egg shells

As the storm roared
Soon, the deed would be done
Since he wanted to stay
Grabbing her fold-up umbrella
Fishing in his pocket for keys
Pressing a hand to her chest
Rubbing the back of his neck
Sunlight dancing on the lake
Sneaking back into the house
Trying not to squint
Leaving the umbrella by the door
After months of hospital care
Three hours passed a five o'clock shadow
Sunlight poured in
Before he reached the front door

Good transition sentences for moving from one scene to the next.

As he tossed his keys
As the air thinned
As the pavement turned to gravel
When the train arrived several minutes later
Thirty minutes later
The next day
At noon on Monday
Early the next morning
By the time five o'clock arrived
That afternoon
Later that afternoon
As the workday wound down
Back in the car
Back on the road again
When light began to fade
When the sun began to set
When the moon began to rise

Despite the long drive
Despite the six-hour drive
It only took thirty minutes
By the time she got the car parked
Later in the week
Later, over beer and pizza
In their Saturday morning habit
By early afternoon

Don't you think those examples in the first section are a more interesting way to start sentences than Maggie smiled, Maggie frowned, Jace shook his head, or Jace narrowed his eyes?

Okay, you get the point, which brings me to the next point. It's perfectly fine to use those two word starts, especially if you're identifying your speaker so you won't have to use a tag/attribution... *he said, she said.* But if you overdo it, they become posturing. You're just using the action of smiling or frowning to keep from using a tag...and that's just as bad.

However, if you add some introspection, it flows better. Here are a few examples of what I mean.

First without it...*Maggie smiled. "May I come in?"*

Now let's add just a bit or introspection.

Maggie smiled. The one that always got results. "May I come in?"

Jace narrowed his eyes. "I don't think so."

Jace narrowed his eyes and his frown said it wasn't working. "I don't think so."

Since we're in Maggie's POV, she's the one who has to determine what Jace is thinking....*no sale.*

It could have been written like this.

Jace narrowed his eyes and his frown warned her he wasn't about to trust her.

OR...*Jace narrowed his eyes, and his frown said he wasn't buying it.*

Enough of the writing rules.....drumroll ......and now to the lists.

BODY
(Action)

Ache
Bend
Burn
Contort
Cower
Cringe
Crouch
Crumble
Curl
Dance
Fidget
Go/went limp
Go/went rigid
Heat
Hug
Jitter
Kneel
Lean
Lunge
Perspired
Posed
Press
Quiver
Recoil
Relax
Sag
Settle
Shake
Shiver
Shook
Shudder
Slouch

Slump
Spin
Squat
Squirm
Stagger
Steadied
Stiffen
Stoop
Stretch
Sway
Sweat
Swung
Teeter
Tighten
Totter
Twirl
Twist
Warm
Weave
Wince
Yielded

(Description)

Agile
Alluring
Anorexic
Arched back
Bare
Broad
Bronzed
Buff
Burly
Cat-like
Chunky
Cold
Compact
Delicate
Doughy
Elegant
Exquisite
Fat
Firm
Flabby
Flexible
Frantic
Gangly
Glorious
Gorgeous
Graceful
Hard
Heavy
Hot
Hour-glass
Husky
Imposing
Jittery
Lean
Leathery
Limp
Lissome
Lithe
Little
Muscular
Naked
Nimble
Obese
Olive skinned
Overweight
Petite
Plum
Plump
Powerful
Pudgy
Reedy
Round
Rugged
Scrawny
Sculpted
Slender
Slight
Slim
Splendid
Squatty
Stacked
Stiff
Stout
Strong
Sturdy
Supple
Svelte

Tanned	Trim
Taut	Uneasy
Thick	Voluptuous
Thin	Willowy
Tiny	

Here are some examples of how to use action and description to break up dialogue. In this first excerpt, we use an action for the body and shoulders, and a description and action for eyes.

From Tied With a Bow and No Place to Go.

*Doyle **shifted in his seat, then squared his shoulders**. "I don't care if it's appraised at ten million dollars, if you can't sell it for estimated value, then it's worthless. It may be good on paper, but I won't get anywhere near the assessed amount. Matter of fact, I could be stuck with paying taxes on it for years. How long do you think it'd take to eat up any profit I'd make? Bottom line . . ." His **dark eyes narrowed**. "I didn't kill Jay Roy for his land. I'm as sad as anyone over his death. We were friends."*

In this excerpt there's action of the body... slumping, feet... toeing out of boots, and action plus description of his neck...rolling and stiff.

From Tell Me a Secret

*He slung his bag onto the desk, **slumped into the chair,
toed out of his boots, then rolled his stiff neck.** The
evening had gone perfectly. If Maggie thought she could
make the rules—well, she had a lot to learn. He'd been
manipulating girls since age thirteen, and now at twenty-
three, he had it down to a science. Of course, it didn't hurt
to have inside information.*

Another example from Tell Me a Secret

This one shows how an animal can help out with emotions.
Through the dialogue Jace has with his pet, we find out
Jace is anxious to see Maggie. If it was a normal reaction
for humans, Jace's whole body would be shaking, too!

Heisman ran back and dropped the stick again.

*"You ready to see Maggie? You ready to see her?" He
cupped the dog's muzzle and gave it a shake, causing him
to wag his tail so hard, his **whole body shook**. "Yeah, me
too, boy."*

SKIN

(Action)

Blush
Burned
Chilled
Cooled
Crawled
Flamed
Flushed
Heated
Inflamed
Itched
Prickled
Redden
Tighten
Tingle
Warmed

(Description)

Aged
Ashy
Bare
Blotchy
Bronzed
Bruised
Clammy
Cold
Colorless
Creamy
Dark
Drawn
Dry
Fair
Flabby

Flawless
Flushed
Freckled
Leathery
Mocha
Moist
Pale
Pallid
Pasty
Rough
Satin
Sensitive
Shiny
Sickly
Smooth

Spotty	Wan
Sunburnt	Washed out
Supple	Waxen
Sweaty	Wet
Taut	White
Tender	Wrinkled
Velvety	Youthful

You're Busting My Nuptials

*The candles flamed up and hissed. Tizzy focused on the woman's face, her **black skin shining like patent leather shoes** on Sunday morning.*

Tell Me a Secret

*Logging off the computer, she closed her journal, crossed the room to the bureau and removed red silk pajamas. The **fabric slid against smooth skin** and the color red made her feel sexy. A glass of wine was a good idea, so she went into the kitchen, took a stemmed goblet from the cupboard and a bottle of Cabernet from the wine rack.*

Two Wrongs Make a Right

*The reflection in the mirror confirmed she looked as bad as she felt. Dark circles ringed beneath her eyes, **and taut, pale skin stretched as tight as a pair of Spanx.** She splashed cold water on her cheeks, blotted her face dry, and ran a brush through her hair.*

HAIR
(Action)

Blow
Bounce
Cascade
Curl
Dangle
Drape
Droop
Fall/fell
Flip
Float
Flow
Fly
Fly away
Frizz

Glinted
Hang
Kink
Shine/Shone
Spill
Spread
Stick out
Sway
Swing
Trail
Tumbled
Twist
Wave

(Description)

Afro
Ash
Auburn
Backcombed
Bald
Bald spot
Bangs
Beehive
Big
Big-bar (a Texas thang)
Black
Bleached
Blonde
Blow-dried
Bobbed
Bottle-blonde
Bouffant

Braided
Brown
Brushed
Bun
Bushy
Butch
Buzz-cut
Chignon
Close-cropped
Close-cut
Coiffed
Combed
Comb-over
Copper
Cornrows
Crew-cut
Curly

Damp
Dark
Dirty
Disheveled
Drab
Dreadlocks
Dyed
Dye job
Finger combed
Fiery-orange
Fiery-red
Fixed
Fluffed
French twist
Fringed
Frosted
Glossy
Gorgeous
Greasy
Grey
Highlighted
Honey-colored
Honey-wheat
In place
Inky
Kinky
Layered
Long
Loose
Mane
Matted
Midnight
Mohawk
Mop
Mullet
Neat
Oily

Permed
Pig-tails
Plaited
Plastered
Ponytail
Ratted
Raven
Receding
Red
Ringlets
Salt and pepper
Shaggy
Shiny
Short
Shoulder-length
Silky
Silver
Sleek
Slick
Spiked
Straight
Streaked
Swept
Swept back
Tangled
Thin
Tied-up
Tousled
Tresses
Trimmed
Unruly
Up-do
Wavy
Weaved
Wet
Wheat-colored
White

Widow's peak   Windblown
Wild

From Two Wrongs Make a Right

*Raynie released her and stepped back. "What's wrong with him?" Grabbing Quinn's shoulders she spun her around. "What's not to love? Dark brown eyes. **Midnight hair.** I'd kill for your looks. Besides, in my profession, people expect me to be exotic."*

"With my pale skin, not sure I consider myself exotic, but whatever I am, it isn't the look Brad wants."

*Quinn turned to face her. She should be so lucky. Megan married her high school sweetheart, and Charlie was one of the best men on the planet. If anyone deserved him, it was Megan. She raked a **long auburn curl** behind her ear, and Quinn eyed her with envy. The **red-haired beauty** always looked great. Even now, without a drop of makeup, her skin glowed and her blue eyes sparkled with intense interest.*

*In contrast, Raynie rotated husbands like a circus carousel. What man could resist a **blonde with emerald eyes**, not to mention her perfectly portioned body? She twirled around, her tiered skirt swishing with the movement, and the eyelet ruffle on her off the shoulder blouse, fluttered in concert. "I should do a reading." She rummaged in her purse and produced her deck of Tarot cards.*

That's two examples of how physical description can be introduced. Raynie gets in Quinn's description, and in return, through introspection of the POV character, Quinn, we find out how Raynie and Megan look.

In this one, I have Dak notice her hair as a way to transition into his thoughts about her.

*He set his briefcase down and stepped deeper into the room. **Her long dark hair fanned out** over the throw pillow she'd propped under her head. Her chest rose and fell in a steady rhythm. One hand rested on the baby bump, and the other hung off the edge of the sofa. Looking at her caused a lump in his throat. He didn't love her. He couldn't. He wouldn't.*

From Tell Me a Secret

*A strand of **unruly hair** fell into her eyes and she puffed it away, then slid her glasses up on her nose and decided to look on the bright side. Given Jace's reputation, he'd never stick with tutoring and she'd be off the hook. Besides, helping a self-centered pretty boy pass anatomy was the last thing she wanted to do.*

*He walked around the table, dragged a chair out and spoke into her ear. "So we're even now, right?" **The fragrance of her hair**, a mixture of mint and vanilla assaulted him.*

HEAD

(Action)

Ache
Angle
Bang
Bob
Bow
Cock
Dip
Drop
Fall back
Flung back
Hang
Hurt
Lift
Loll
Lower
Nod
Poke
Pound
Press
Raise
Rest
Shake
Slant
Snap
Spin
Swam
Sweat

Throb
Throw back
Tilt
Tip
Toss
Turn
Twist
Wag
Waggle
Way

(Description)

Big
Crown
Fat
Hard
Head over heels
Held high
Huge
Knuckle
Large
Little
Noddle
Noggin
Pumpkin
Small
Tiny

From Tell Me a Secret

*How'd it go?" Sam stood in the doorway with one towel wrapped around his waist and **rubbed his head** with another. His **brown hair curled** into little ringlets and formed a line of perfect commas above his brows.*

In that excerpt, we're in Jace's point of view, so he can comment on any physical description of his roommate, Sam.

When describing characters, think of how you describe yourself...as if in your point of view....because you are. All your thoughts and opinions come from your POV. You never refer to your hair or eye color when you think of yourself. You never say, my brown hair won't do a thing today. You simply say, my hair won't do a thing today. Same with eyes.

So your point of view character will never think that way either. They won't push a strand of dark brown hair behind their ear. Or widen their green eyes. You must figure out another way to work in their description. It usually comes from another's point of view as they look at the other character, OR through dialogue, as with Raynie, Megan, and Quinn in a previous example, but there are other ways.

Here are a couple of examples of how to do that.

From Tell Me a Secret

Maggie's heart pounded. Stomach churned. Time passed with no significance. She didn't remember going into the bathroom. But now at the sink, she splashed cold water on her face and gazed at the reflection in the mirror. **Almost the image of her mother, barely five-foot-three and a hundred pounds, but the family genes of voluptuous curves and full rounded breasts skipped Maggie's generation. Instead, she'd gotten cursed with fiery hair,** *which most of the time looked as if an explosion had occurred.*

In this excerpt, without "telling" Maggie is five-feet-three, with red hair and small boobs, we learn her height and that she has wild, red hair, a slight body, and small breasts . Looking in a mirror is a way to do that, but the character must be comparing herself to someone else in order for it to work, or it will still come across as the POV character telling her own description...which is a big no-no.

Here's one more example.

From my current work in progress:

Other than the sharp nose she'd gotten from her dad, Silbie was the spitting image of her mom and aunt. **Same green eyes, honey-blonde hair, mischievous smile.** *Raynie could pass for her mother, but she wasn't, and the worst part? She didn't know how to be.*

Later in the story, Raynie's love interest will think about how she looks, but this is in the first chapter, so to give the reader a good sense of my female lead early on, I introduce her description by comparison to her niece.

In the below excerpt from Two Wrongs Make a Right, the main character is seeing Justin for the first time. She's already described him to the reader earlier in the story...dark hair, killer dimples, so now she concentrates on how he's dressed. Just in case you don't know what "stacked" jeans means...it's where men buy them longer than they need, so when they wear them...they *stack*. Think country singer, George Strait!

For the past few days, she'd propped his picture on her dresser and practiced conversation with him. Now, every thought evaporated. Wearing a plaid sport shirt, jeans starched and stacked above cowboy boots, he was more handsome than the company photo. Her mouth went dry and then Molly reminded her. Of course we're turned on, we're ovulating.

EYES

(Action)

Adjusted
Appraise
Avert
Betrayed
Blaze
Blink
Blurred
Brighten
Brow lifted
Brow raised
Brows arched
Brows knit
Bulge
Calculating
Caressed
Cat-like
Close
Closed
Crease
Crinkle
Cross
Dart
Dim
Drank in
Dropped
Examined
Exotic
Eyeballed
Fix
Flame
Flash
Flicker
Flit
Flutter
Flutter lashes
Furrow brow
Gape
Gawk
Gaze
Glance
Glazed
Gleam
Glint
Glow
Half-close
Inspected
Intense
Jump
Knit brows
Latch
Leer
Lock
Lower
Lowered
Melted
Moisten
Nailed
Narrow
Ogle
Opened
Peeked
Peeped
Peered
Pierced
Ping-pong
Pop
Probed
Protrude

Raise brow
Reflected
Regarded
Roamed
Roll/ Rolled
Scrutinize
Search
Settle
Shimmer
Shine
Shut
Sinister
Sized up
Skimmed
Slanted
Smolder
Sparked
Sparkled

Spied
Squeeze
Squinted
Stared
Steady
Studied
Surveyed
Swept
Train
Twinkled
Twitch
Unblinking
Undressed
Water
Widen
Wink
Witnessed

(Description)

Ablaze
Alert
Almond
Amber
Azure
Baby-blue
Beady
Bedroom
Bewildered
Black
Bloodshot
Blue
Blue-green
Brown
Bug-eyed
Bulging

Calm
Caustic
Cerulean
Charcoal
Chocolate
Clear
Coal
Cold
Cruel
Dazzling
Deep-set
Devilish
Doe-eyed
Dreamy
Dull
Eager

Ebony
Electric
Emerald
Fiery
Gloomy
Gray
Green
Half-lidded
Hazel
Hollow
Hot
Hungry
Ice blue
Intense
Jade
Lazy
Lust-filled
Mischievous
Mysterious
Narrow
Obsidian
Pale
Piercing

Resentful
Restless
Roguish
Round
Sad
Sapphire
Sky blue
Slanted
Smoky
Smoldering
Snake eyes
Spaced evenly
Stern
Stone cold
Sympathetic
Teary
Tired
Tortured
Violet
Weary
Whiskey-colored
Wicked
Wide

Here's an example of where I overwrote. Also some action for eyes, and description for fingers.

From Tied With a Bow and No Place to Go

*When the man gave her the balls, Tizzy **eyed his fingers.** "Those are interesting tattoos."*

*He **glanced at his hands**, back at her, and then focused on the logo stitched across Rayann's tank top. His eyes went wide ~~with panic~~. Opening the door behind him, he ran from the ticket booth, and disappeared into the crowd.*

Earlier in the story, I'd established the tattoos play an important part. Because of that, the reader knows the guy will panic when Tizzy makes that statement, therefore, his eyes going wide, and then running away shows the reader his panic without me (the author) telling them.

Here's an example of how a simile shows description, action and emotion.

From Laid Out and Candle Lit

"Wouldn't want to traumatize Gracie, in case she wakes up." ***His eyes gleamed like a Coyote that'd just found a nest of baby ducks.*** *"You did say anything. Right?"*

Eyes and hands are probably the most used body parts in a story to convey action and emotion, both in dialogue and narrative. Here's another example.

Excerpt from Two Wrongs Make a Right

*He turned to look at her again, this time **holding her gaze** longer. For a moment, something **flashed in his eyes**. It was in those seconds, the real Dak surfaced. He was still in there, buried under the anger and hurt. If she could hold out long enough, maybe good Dak would win out over bitter Dak.*

TEARS

(Action)

Brimmed
Downpour
Dropped
Edged
Erupted
Fell
Flooded
Flowed
Gushed
Leaked
Poured
Ran
Rimmed
Rolled
Rushed
Seeped
Spill
Sprang
Streamed
Stung
Surged
Threatened
Trailed
Waited
Waned
Welled

(Description)

Bloody
Burned
Crocodile
Fake
Glistened
Hot
Pretend
Profuse
Salty
Warm

From Laid Out and Candle Lit

*Rayann blotted her cheeks, then pulled down the visor mirror and removed the marks. "No. If he is cheating, I can't discuss it with him." She **erupted into tears** again. "You see how upset I get just talking to you?"*

Again, by mixing in some action or description among dialogue, it sounds more natural. We rarely just sit or stand motionless and blank while we talk. Most of the time, we're doing other things, making gestures, and expressions along with conversation, even if it's only to fold our arms or shift our weight from side to side.

Pay attention to your actions while conversing, or watch other people, then put it in your story!

From You're Busting My Nuptials

*Tizzy **tapped her chest with her fingers**. "For some reason, I can't. I feel like all my **tears are stuck** right here and they won't budge." She took an unsteady breath and faced her two best friends. "C'mon, let's go find Ridge."*

From Tell Me a Secret

Maggie tossed and turned, fluffed her pillow, kicked off the cover, rolled to her left, and then her right. Finally, she flopped onto her back, gently rubbed her belly, and admitted what she'd feared all along.

*At first, **she cried** softly and then **tears** came harder and faster, until she grabbed the extra pillow and covered her face to drown her moans. Once the **downpour** ended, she told herself to think logically and consider the facts.*

NOSE

(Action)

Blew/blow
Breathed
Buried
Burned
Dripped
Exhale
Flared
Inhale
Itched
Nosedived

Press against/to
Raise
Smelled
Sniffed
Sniveled
Snuffled
Stuck in the air
Tickle
Twitch
Wiggle
Wrinkle

(Description)

Aquiline
Aristocratic
Arrogant
Beak
Bent
Big
Bloody
Bold
Broad
Brown nosed
Bulbous
Button
Crooked
Curved
Cute
Dainty
Delicate
Elegant
Enormous
Flat
Freckled

Grecian
Honker
Hooked
Huge
Large
Long
Narrow
Nose in the air
Perfect
Pert
Pig-like
Pointed
Pointy
Roman
Runny
Snitcher
Snout
Snubbed
Straight
Swollen
Thin
Turned up

According to statistics, the most powerful sense to use in a story is smell. It plays the biggest part in setting a scene. Just the mention of home baked bread, the scent of vanilla, or how a little kid smells after playing outside in hot weather, can conjure up memories from a reader's past. So when you're writing your locations, have your characters describe what they smell, as well as what they see.

Here are examples of how smell can help set a scene.

From Tell Me a Secret

The dorm reeked of dirty socks and burly football players. *He toed out of his boots. "We got off to a bad start. I showed up late. It went downhill from there."*

From Laid Out and Candle Lit

*When he stepped inside, **the strong stench of bleach** caused his breath to catch and his eyes to burn. Someone definitely expected the cabin to be checked out.*

Bubba cleared his throat and wiped his nose. "Someone did some serious cleaning. What do you bet we aren't going to find much evidence?"

Another excerpt from Laid Out and Candle Lit

*Hours later, along with Bubba, Ridge stood on the porch and stared across the lake. The **smell of honeysuckle and wild privet caused his nose to twitch.***

Even if I'd not already established the time of year in the story, by this excerpt, the reader would know it's summer time because of the odors.

From Two Wrongs Make a Right

*For just a bit of fortitude, she grabbed a shot from the table and knocked it back, hoping tequila and banana mixed well together. Holy crap. The **inside of her nose went cold.** At least it opened her sinuses.*

I could have stopped after the sentence…The inside of her nose went cold, but by adding that bit of introspection, it gives the paragraph more punch and tells us that the character has some humor about her.

From Tell Me a Secret

*Uncle Charles' office, on the eleventh floor of the only high rise in downtown, was as big as a banquet hall. The walls, paneled in opulent dark mahogany and varnished to a rich gloss, lent a bronzed light to the room. **It smelled of leather, wood, and whiskey,** his drink of choice. A wall of windows provided a view of the city's skyline.*

CHEEKS

(Action)	(Description)
Burned	Apples
Colored	Chubby
Dimpled	Crinkly
Flamed	Dimpled
Flush	Fat
Heated	Full
Paled	High cheek bones
Puffed out	Passion-red
Redden	Pink
Suck in	Pock-marked
Tingled	Puffed
Turned pink	Red
	Round
	Ruddy
	Sallow
	Scarred
	Smooth
	Soft
	Swollen
	Sunken
	Tinged

From Two Wrongs Make a Right

*She **rubbed their ears**. "Yes. There're two of us. Both crazy. I'm practicing my alluring moves. Good or not?" She **pursed her lips and fluttered her lashes**. The cats stared, frozen in place. "Yeah. That's what I thought. More sick than sexy. How am I ever going to tempt a man if I look like I'm in the middle of a seizure?"*

*As if answering, Lucy **nudged Ethel with her nose, then
ran her tongue across her head.** "What? I should **lick**
him? Maybe after I get him into bed."* Her **cheeks heated,**
*and the tattoo on the side of Rico's neck flashed in her
mind. Very lickable. She flapped her hands at the cats.
"You girls get out of here. You're a bad influence." They
sprang to the floor and disappeared down the hallway.*

Lots of different body parts with action in those paragraphs,
and it brings up another thing I do in my novels. My
characters always have a pet. If they don't when the story
begins, they will before it ends.

Animals provide a chance to reveal things to your reader
without actually introducing more characters. Not that a
large number of players is a bad thing, but too many in one
chapter, can muddy the water. Besides, having one sided
conversation is easier than writing complicated dialogue!

Same thing with kids. Children provide opportunities in a
story for some humor and a different type of dialogue.

LIPS/MOUTH

(Action)

Angle
Blow
Brush
Catch between teeth
Chew
Clamp shut
Clench
Close
Corners turn up
Cover
Crush
Curl
Demand
Devour
Down turn
Dribble
Drool
Drop open
Edge up at corners
Entice
Explored
Fall/fell open
Forced smile
Frown
Gape
Gasp
Grimace
Grin
Half-smiled
Hung on
Hung open
Hover

Laugh
Lower
Mouthed
Open
Parted
Pouted
Pressed
Pucker
Pursed
Quirk up
Quiver
Relax
Rub against
Sip
Skimmed
Smile
Smirk
Sneer
Spit
Suck
Surrender
Swallow
Taste
Thin
Thrust
Tighten
Tingle
Tremble
Twisted
Twitched
Watered
Words fall/fell from/out

Wrap around
Yawn
Zipped

(Description)

Addictive
Alluring
Attractive
Beautiful
Big-mouthed
Blabber-mouthed
Chapped
Cracked
Curved
Delicious
Dry
Eager
Firm
Frog-like
Full
Generous
Glossy
Goh
Gorgeous
Handsome
Heart-shaped
Hot
Hungry
Kissable
Little
Lower
Luscious
Lush
Moist
Painted
Parched
Petite
Pie hole
Pillow
Potty-mouthed
Pouty
Pretty
Ripe
Rosy
Salacious
Sculpted
Sensuous
Sexy
Sinful
Soft
Succulent
Sweet
Swollen
Thick
Thin
Upper
Warm
Wet
Wicked
Willing

From Two Wrongs Make a Right

She hesitated and drew a shallow breath. "See, I was right. I've shamed you into saying that. I should go back to my..."

*Dak yanked her closer and **crushed his mouth** down on hers. At first, she went rigid, then clutched his shirt to pull him tighter against her. He **hung on to the kiss,** and the heart blip became a full blown arrhythmia. By the time their **lips parted,** she'd gone limp. He kept his hands around her waist for fear she might collapse onto the pavement.*

She struggled for breath and he pulled her even tighter. He'd hold her all night if he had to.

From Laid Out and Candle Lit

*It'd been years since they shared a **kiss.** She thought it would be familiar. But it wasn't. This wasn't the kiss of a naïve, doubtful, eighteen year old. This kiss was powerful, demanding. This kiss laid claim. Not only to her **mouth** and tongue, but to her very soul.*

In romance, readers want to know what the characters feel and think about the other, so when they have a scene together, there needs to be details as to what hands, lips, heart, and any other body part involved is doing! Look at everything going on in the first example.

She's having trouble breathing.
His lips crush hers.
The kiss is so unexpected, she stiffens.
But as it goes on, she likes it.
He doesn't want it to end, so he draws it out.
He likes it so much his heart goes wild.
By the time it ends, she's as limp as a dishrag.
He holds on, because he doesn't want to let her go.
He's willing to hold her all night if necessary.

I could have written it like the above summary. Choppy sentences, less pronouns and words. It gives the same information, but it's not nearly as interesting. Another of my many flaws... I write pronoun heavy. I continue to work on the problem, but it's a hard habit to break. So, do as I say, not as I do, and try to write sentences without a lot of he, she, her, him!

This is a good place to mention some sites I find helpful in editing. Editminion.com will check for several things, like repeat words, passive voice, etc. It's simple and free to use. Just copy and paste your chapter into their template. There is a word limit, so pay attention to that. It's worth a try.

Another editing tool is ProWritingAid.com. They have limited use for free, and yearly memberships where the software checks more things. Repeat words, passive voice, grammar, punctuation, etc. In some instances, they suggest changes. It works well with Word, and the cost is about $35.00 per year.

TEETH

(Action)

Ache
Bite
Catch lip between
Chatter
Chew
Chomped
Clamped
Clenched
Clink
Gnash
Graze
Grind
Grit
Ground
Lied through
Nip
Sink
Snap

(Description)

Bare
Big
Braces
Brilliant
Broken
Brown
Buckteeth
Chipped
Crooked
Dazzling
Even
False
Front
Gleam
Glittering
Horse teeth
Large
Pearly
Perfect
Rabbit
Sharp
Shiny
Snaggle-toothed
Stained
Straight
Tobacco stained
Toothless
White
Yellow

From Tell Me a Secret

As other couples performed, Jace couldn't keep his mind on their routines thinking instead of how Marc touched Maggie. Jace didn't like it. Not one bit. ***A pain shot up his cheek and he realized he'd been grinding his teeth. He rubbed a hand across his jaw bone.***

In this excerpt, I am *telling* that Jace doesn't like Maggie being touched by Marc, even if they are in a dance recital. I could have just shown the emotion by the pain shooting up his cheek and the grinding of teeth. However, stories need a bit of telling, again, sprinkled in.

From You're Busting My Nuptials

"I did what Nana said." Gracie thrust her fingers forward into blank space. "I poked him." She snapped her leg out. "I kicked him." She made a chomping sound and clicked her **teeth together.** *"And* **I bit him.**"

See that bit of overwriting? Is there any other kind of space than blank? Not sure I needed "blank" in that sentence.

TONGUE

(Action)

Assault
Breach
Caress
Circle
Coil
Connect
Consumed
Curl
Dance
Dart
Devour
Dip
Discover
Dive
Drag
Examine
Explore
Extend
Flick
Jab
Lash
Laved
Lick
Move
Plunder
Plunge
Point
Poke
Probe
Prod
Run over lips
Slide
Stick out
Stimulate
Stroke
Swirl
Take
Taste
Taunt
Tease
Touch
Toy
Twine
Wag

(Description)

Hot
Lizard-like
Magic
Relentless
Seductive
Skilled
Skillful
Slippery
Velvet
Warm
Wet

From Tell Me a Secret

*I hadn't French kissed a boy since Eric Jenkins in eighth grade. I remember it being gross. His **tongue inside my mouth felt how I imagined a lizard's. Pointy, slimy.***

From Two Wrongs Make a Right

*As the cab pulled from the curb, Quinn opened one of the to-go boxes, removed a Madeleine, and shoved it into her mouth. The cake felt like **sawdust on her tongue**. She stared out the window at passing cars, **licked her lips** and tasted salty tears. Damn him. She sniffed, wiped them away with the sleeve of her jacket, and reminded herself crying was useless. It was over, and that, was that.*

From Tied With a Bow and No Place to Go

*As Tizzy put the car in gear and headed for the highway, she figured by now, all over town, **tongues were wagging** about Jay Roy. He'd been a lifetime member of the community, a star quarterback in high school, and current owner of a string of chicken houses.*

CHIN

(Action)

Dip
Drop to chest
Jut
Keep up
Pull down
Pull in
Quiver
Thrust out
Tilt down
Tilt up
Tremble

(Description)

Bearded
Boney
Cleft
Determined
Dimpled
Double
Flabby
Hairy
Pointed
Prominent
Sharp
Square
Strong
Stubbly
Stubborn
Weak
Wrinkled

From Laid Out and Candle Lit

Tizzy set the plates down. "One of these days, Bubba, you're going to find a woman who melts you like butter." She glanced over her shoulder toward Rayann.

He jutted out his chin. *"Maybe I've already found her. Have you thought about that?"*

From Tell Me a Secret

He appeared to shift into slow motion, his stride lyrical, as if shuffling to a soulful beat leaving no doubt as to why girls found him irresistible. He looked as if he could take you to hell, and you'd enjoy the trip. Leaner than the men in her fantasies, he had the same blue eyes and dark hair, and a **small paper-thin scar on his chin** *made him just dangerous enough.*

Normally a scar might be considered a bad thing, but in the above passage, Maggie even finds that flaw appealing. Although I tried not to make Jace perfect, somehow, she still thought he was!

One more from Tell Me a Secret

Maggie pushed away again and rested her **chin** *in her hand. "I have one more secret."*

FACE

(Action)

Betrayed
Blushed
Burned
Composed
Contorted
Darkened
Deadpan
Drained
Draw into hard line
Frowned
Glow
Grimace
Guarded
Light
Paled
Pinch
Screwed up
Screwed-around
Scrunched
Tensed
Tilt
Twisted

(Description)

Aged
Amused
Angelic
Angry
Angular
Baby-faced
Beautiful
Bewildered
Blank

Blotchy
Carved
Cheerful
Child-like
Chiseled
Chubby
Clear
Composed
Crabby

Craggy
Cynical
Delicate
Drawn
Dreamy
Fatigued
Fine
Flawless
Flinty
Freckled
Fresh
Full-face
Furrowed
Gaunt
Giddy
Glum
Good looking
Grave
Grim
Haggard
Handsome
Happy
Hard
Hatchet
Icy
Innocent
Lined
Made-up
Mug
Old

Oval
Pale
Pasty
Pock-marked
Porcelain
Puzzled
Reluctant
Ruddy
Rugged
Sad
Scarred
Seamed
Skeptical
Sculpted
Smooth
Steely
Strained
Sullen
Tanned
Thoughtful
Tired
Two-faced
Ugly
Unhappy
Unlined
Wary
Weak
Weather-beaten
Wrinkled
Youthful

Two excerpts from Laid Out and Candle Lit

*She pressed **fingertips to temples** and made small circles. THINK, THINK, THINK, DAMMIT! In one motion, she **launched her body upright.** Dizzy from the sudden move, she leaned forward and **placed her head between her knees.** She **fanned her face with both hands.** DON'T THROW UP, DON'T THROW UP, NOT ON YOUR WEDDING DRESS.*

*The bulky woman relaxed back in the chair and loosened her hands. Beads of **sweat rolled down her cheeks.** She pulled a handkerchief from between her bosom and mopped her face.*

The face shows a lot about a character. Even though each part...eyes, nose, cheeks, can add to the emotion sometimes simply mopping or fanning conveys what the author is trying to show.

From Tell Me a Secret

*She sat up, grabbed her phone and checked the weather again. "This time tomorrow, the roads should be clear enough for travel." She picked the cat up and dangled her until they were **face to face.** "Twenty-four hours. I only have to make it twenty-four hours. I can do that."*

NECK

(Action)

Ache
Adam's apple bob
Adam's apple jerk
Arch
Bent
Burn
Crane
Heat
Redden
Roll
Snap
Stiffen
Strain
Stretch
Swivel
Tense
Twist
Warmed

(Description)

Broad
Creamy
Delicate
Elegant
Elongated
Fat
Flabby
Goose
Graceful
Long
Loose skin
Muscular
Regal
Saggy
Stiff
Swan-like
Tanned
Tattooed
Thick
Throat
Warm
Windpipe
Wrinkled

Most of the time *neck* is used in the context of hands running around it, or any of those actions listed above…scratching, craning, rubbing, rolling, etc. or hair raising on the back of it, but sometimes it can provide a location for some other action to happen, like in the first excerpt. In the next two, it serves as part of a series of actions.

It can also provide a place for a character to grab… the neck of someone's shirt, or remove a scarf.

Three excerpts from Tied With a Bow and No Place to Go

Ridge glared at the man and added steel to his voice. "Sit, Mr. Sparks. I'm not done with my questions."

*Sparks sat. The **blood vessels in his neck popped out**, and his pink cheeks reddened.*

*She ran a hand along the side of her cheek, **trailed it to her neck**, finally letting it rest on her chest. "I don't know."*

Ridge followed the movements. "Aren't you still married?"

"Separated."

*"Happy to help." The voice that drawled from her pouty red lips caught Ridge off guard. She ran a slender finger along the lapel of her purple silk blouse, and back to her throat where she rubbed the diamond cross pendant **resting on her windpipe.***

SHOULDERS

(Action)	(Description)
Bared	Athletic
Braced	Bare
Droop	Beefy
Hunch	Big
Lift	Boney
Lowered	Brawny
Moved	Broad
Nudge	Bulky
Pressed	Creamy
Quake	Delicate
Relaxed	Husky
Rise	Muscled
Rolled	Narrow
Sag	Powerful
Shake	Rounded
Shook	Rugged
Shrug	Satin
Shudder	Scrawny
Slump	Sinewy
Squared	Slumped
Stiffen	Smooth
Stretched	Stiff
Tense	Stout
	Strong
	Sturdy
	Tanned
	Tatted
	Thick
	Toned
	Wide

Two examples from Two Wrongs Make a Right

*The memory of his **broad shoulders**, tight jeans, and inked muscles creeping from his vest, caused activity in Blissville. She bit her bottom lip. Never having been with a tatted bad boy before, it intrigued her. Did he slam a woman up against the wall and just take her? Not by force, but because she wanted it. Lord Jesus. Slammed and taken by invitation sounded good.*

Quinn sat up. "We're getting a lot of weapons here. Two of Swords. Six of Swords. Aren't there any Barbell Billys or Tackling Tommys?"

"That's Old Maid, not Tarot. Now do you want me to do this or not?"

*Raynie's **shoulders slumped**, so Quinn dialed back the sarcasm. "Sorry. I'm being silly. Please continue."*

Here, by showing Raynie's shoulders slumping and Quinn's reaction is a good way to reveal the sarcasm without tagging the Tacking Tommy sentence with one of those lazy telling adverbs…Quinn said sarcastically.

CHEST

(Action)

Ache
Brush against
Expand
Heat
Press
Puff out
Seize up
Swell
Tighten
Trembled
Twisted
Warm

(Description)

Athletic
Bare
Broad
Bronzed
Defined
Firm
Hairy
Hard
Impeccable
Masculine
Muscled

Naked
Powerful
Rock hard
Sculpted
Smooth
Solid
Strong
Tan
Taut
Thick
Waxed

Tell Me a Secret

*An old familiar burn started in the pit of her stomach, **rose to her chest** and squeezed the air from her lungs. A sensation she'd not experienced since age sixteen while crushing over Daniel Radcliffe in a Harry Potter Marathon Movie weekend.*

*He held the pages to **his chest** as if to let the words soak into his heart. He pulled them away and read them again.*

*She **pulled her knees to her chest.** "One theory is they're lonely and they want to hear other dogs answer. Some think they're calling their mate, and some imagine it's their way of praying. I googled it." Then she rolled to her knees, took another long sip, and said, "Let's howl at the moon."*

I should have edited the above passage better. I could have left off *and said.* There are only two people in the scene, so by saying she rolled to her knees, the reader knows it's Maggie and the following sentence belonged to her without me telling them...*she said.*

I don't think I ever read anything of mine that I don't see more things to change!!

BREASTS

(Action)
Ache
Bounce
Dangle
Harden
Heat
Heave
Jiggle
Jut
Press
Sag
Skim
Spilled out
Stand at attention
Taunt
Tease
Tense
Throb
Tighten
Tremble
Warm

(Description)
Augmented
Bare
Big
Blobs
Bodacious Ta-Ta's
Boobies
Boobs
Bosom
Boulders
Busty
Butter bags
Butter-bags
Creamy
Delicious
Double D's
Dumplings

Fake
Firm
Full rounded
Full rounded
Headlights
Hooters
Hot
Jugs
Knockers
Large
Love bubbles
Luscious
Magnificent
Massive
Melons
Milky
Mounds
Mouth watering
Naked
Natural
Orbs
Peaks
Perfect
Perky
Pert
Pert
Plump
Puppies
Ripe
Sensitive
Small
Soft
Superdroopers
Sweet
Swells
Swollen
Ta-Ta's
Taut
Tender
The girls
The twins
Tig-bitties
Tits
Voluptuous

Tell Me a Secret

He laughed and scooted lower until flat against the mattress. "Tell me a secret while you're drunk."

*She pulled the neck of her pajamas away from her body and peered inside the top. **"I wish my boobs were bigger."***

*He snorted a laugh so hard the bed shook. **"Every woman wants bigger boobs.** That's not a secret."*

Her head spun like a balloon caught on a high-line. "Nuh-uh. Some women get reduction mammoplasty to make them smaller."

"Focus, Maggie. Tell me a secret."

"If I do, will you leave?"

"Yes."

From Laid Out and Candle Lit

*Dizzy from the drinks. She lost control of her senses and slurred the words out. "I know you like big **boobs**, and I'm sorry I don't have big ones. It's my fault. When the Lord was handing out **tits**, I thought he said grits, and I said I don't like 'em so don't give me much."*

Normally, Rayann would not be that crude in her speech, but she *is* drunk, so I forgive her!

From Two Wrongs Make a Right

*She tossed her blonde curls for effect and took a deep breath. **Full breasts rose from her low cut scarlet dress,** as if pumping up a bicycle tire. Bicycle. Red bicycle. Damn, I loved that ride. He blinked. Man, if he was imagining his first bike while she was giving him that come-and-get-me look, then he was doing the right thing for sure.*

NIPPLES

(Action)

Bead
Brush against/across
Burn
Harden
Leak
Ooze
Peak
Pebble
Push against
Rise/rose
Sprang/sprung to attention
Stand at attention
Swell
Throb
Tighten
Tingle

(Description)

Areola
Bud
Center
Kernel
Nub
Point
Rosy
Silver dollar
Tip crest
Cherries
Nips

Tell Me a Secret

*The sudden blast of cold air caused Maggie's **nipples to stand at attention** and the result didn't go unnoticed by Jace.*

*She pushed past him and moved to the stairway. Her **nipples no longer stood** at attention, but her breasts rose and fell with each breath.*

He tried to focus on her face. "You want to slap me? Go ahead. Let some of that pent up frustration out."

Her expression changed and he braced for impact. Finally, here it comes, the wrath of Maggie. But instead, she continued in the same tone, but this time with more agitation.

STOMACH

(Action)

Bubble
Burn
Churn
Clench
Contract
Cramp
Drop
Fell
Flip-flopped
Fluttered
Growled
Hurt
Knotted
Lurched
Quivered
Rumbled
Sank
Settled
Shook
Sick to stomach
Stirred
Somersaulted
Tensed
Vaulted

(Description)

Abdomen
Belly
Belly laughed
Below the belt
Big
Bread basket
Creamy
Flabby
Flat
Gut
Insides
Jelly-like
Paunch
Pot-belly
Protruded
Queasy
Ripped
Sculpted
Slim
Smooth
Solar plexus
Spare tire
Tanned
Taut
Tense
Tight
Toned
Trim
Tummy
Two bellies
Wash-board
Well-defined

Laid Out and Candle Lit

*A shudder ran up Tizzy's spine and back down. **Bile rose from her stomach.** She fought to keep it down. "Why? I didn't want her dead."*

You're Busting My Nuptials

*Ridge's mother, Hazel, along with his sister, Erica, approached and Tizzy rose to face them while her **stomach somersaulted.***

Tied With a Bow and No Place to Go

*As Ridge pulled into the police lot, **excitement bubbled in his stomach** at the possibility of closing the case with a confession. However, when Bubba called, he didn't seem to share that emotion. That made Ridge uneasy and suspicious.*

Two Wrongs Make a Right

*The announcement had her blinking and wondering why she didn't slap him. "Are you kidding me? You want me to buy your condo?" **Fire burned in the pit of her stomach like she'd swallowed a hot coal.***

Tell Me a Secret

*On December twenty-sixth, the sky, blanketed with low, gray clouds held the rush of icy wind close to the ground. Naked trees twisted and turned, their limbs dancing to the rhythm of the currents. Maggie stiffened in her seat, **stomach twirling and twining** with them. Pulling her coat tighter, a chill ran up her spine, not from the elements, but from the truth that waited.*

Again, from Tell Me a Secret

*Maggie tossed and turned, fluffed her pillow, kicked off the cover, rolled to her left, and then her right. Finally, she flopped onto her back, gently **rubbed her belly**, and admitted what she'd feared all along.*

At first, she cried softly and then tears came harder and faster, until she grabbed the extra pillow and covered her face to drown her moans. Once the downpour ended, she told herself to think logically and consider the facts.

ARMS

(Action)

Circled
Cling/clung
Closed
Coil
Cradle
Cross
Crushed
Curved
Draped
Dropped
Embrace
Encircled
Flex
Fling
Fold
Gathered
Hang
Hold
Hug
Jerked

Lifted
Linked
Locked
Loop
Opened
Protected
Pulled
Pumped
Pushed
Relaxed
Rested
Scooped
Sheltered
Shivered
Slid
Spread
Stretch
Supported
Swing
Wave
Wrap

(Description)

Beefy
Bulged
Boney
Bronzed
Chiseled
Corded
Defined
Farmer's tan
Flabby
Lean
Muscled

Muscular
Scrawny
Shapely
Sinewy
Skinny
Slender
Smooth
Strong
Tanned
Tatted
Tattooed

Taut	Thin
Thick	Toned

Most of the time we think of arms doing the action…wrapping, holding, swinging, etc. But here are some examples of arms receiving the action in place of providing it.

From Tell Me a Secret

__Flying into his arms__, he lifted and twirled her in the air. When they stopped spinning, he planted her feet back on the tile. "Well?"

Without warning, she __fell into his arms__.

Then she __jumped back into his arms__.

Two Wrongs Make a Right

__And those arms, big and strong__, holding her so tight, escape was impossible, not that she wanted to. Clutching his shirt, to bring him closer, she never wanted the contact to end. This kind of passion had never happened with Brad. Never. How could that be? Why stay in a relationship with someone as bland as oatmeal? Well, not tonight. Nope. She planned to release her inner Molly and set the world on fire. If not the world, at least room 207 at the LaQuinta.

HANDS/FINGERS

(Action)

Accept (handshake)
Ball
Bang
Brace
Bracket
Brush
Bury
Capture
Chuck
Clap
Clasp
Claw
Clench
Close
Clutch
Collect
Cover
Crack
Curl
Dig
Dip
Drag
Drop
Drum
Entwine
Envelope
Extend
Fan
Fan out
Feather over
Feel
Fetch
Fiddle
File
Finger
Fish
Fist
Flap
Flex
Flick
Fling
Fondle
Fumble
Gesture
Glide
Gouge
Grasp
Grip
Grope
Heave
Hoist
Hold
Hook
Hover
Hurl
Intertwine
Jab
Jerk
Knock
Knotted
Lace
Lift

Lob
Lock
Lower
Massage
Move
Palm
Pat
Paw
Pick
Pinch
Pitch
Plant
Point
Poke
Pound
Press
Probe
Pull
Raise
Rake
Rap
Reach
Release
Remove
Replace
Rifle
Roam
Rooted
Rub
Rummage
Run/ran across
Scavenge
Scoop
Scratch
Search
Shake/shook
Shelve

Shove
Sift
Skated over
Skim
Skimmed
Slap
Sling
Smack
Smoothed
Snatch
Splay
Spread
Steeple
Strike
Stroke
Strum
Swat
Sweaty
Tangle
Tap
Thread
Throw
Torment
Toss
Touch
Trail
Tuck
Tug
Twine
Unbutton
Unclench
Unsnap
Waggle
Wave
Whirl
Wring

(Description)

Arthritic
Artistic
Big
Blunt
Boney
Calloused
Chubby
Cold
Comforting
Damp
Delicate
Dirty
Fast
Fine-boned
Freckled
Gentle
Grimy
Grubby
Heavy-handed
Icy
Knarled
Little
Long
Manicured
Meaty
Mitts
Nimble
Powerful
Rough
Scarred
Skilled
Slender
Small
Soft
Spotted
Stiff
Strong
Sun-kissed
Sweaty
Translucent
Velvet
Warm
Wrinkled

Fingers may be my favorite body part to write. They can do so much in so many different ways. I think they are almost as expressive as eyes. Lots of finger action in the example below...pointing, tapping, clicking.

From Tied With a Bow and No Place to Go

*She squinted and **pointed to her glass**. "I wonder why they call this drink Hop, Skip, and Go Naked, because it makes you too tired to do any of those things." Her eyes closed.*

*Ridge **clicked his pen** several times, leaned back against the chair and let the silence hang between them. Then he leaned forward and **tapped her** on the head. "Now let's talk about the mayor's husband."*

From You're Busting My Nuptials

Nana smoothed her hair. "No, I want Om to be a surprise."

*Tizzy twirled the bright umbrella from her drink **between her fingers.** "Oh, he will be." She stuck the paper parasol behind her ear. "Tell me, Nana. What's your plan for Ommmmmmm?"*

"Marjorie Louise, stop saying his name like that. You're being disrespectful," Nana snapped.

"I'm sorry, but you have to admit this is irrational behavior on your part. You're not planning to marry this man, are you?"

Again, in the following sample, fingers receive the action instead of giving it.

From Tell Me a Secret

*He leaned in close and offered her his best smile, then reached over and **played with her fingers.** "What about me? Am I invited?" She swallowed hard and pulled her hand away. The slight touch affected her, but Jace wondered, did she like it—or was she offended?*

In the next sample, you'll see why I love fingers and why I think they rival eyes. Dak is excited by the action Molly provides. I think it's a sensual scene without any graphic sex. In my mind, I can see this play out on the big screen!

From Two Wrongs Make a Right

He held open the door, and she walked in ahead of him, fiddling with her hair. Emory Quinn had already taken the stage and was in the middle of Holes Through the Windows. He nodded toward his friends, then ushered Molly to the dance floor.

*He slipped both hands around her waist. She hooked her thumb in his belt loop, then rested her other hand on his chest, and did the strangest thing. She **circled one of his shirt buttons with her finger**. Around and around, over and over, slow and steady, and his heart lost its rhythm again. About the time normal cadence returned, **she worked the button in and out of its hole.** He tried to pay attention to the words of the song, but that button action was driving him crazy.*

LEGS/FEET

(Action)

Ache
Bounce
Braced
Brushed
Cross
Dance
Dangle
Drag
Entwined
Fold
Jitter
Kick
Lifted
March
Moved
Opened
Parted
Positioned
Propped up
Raise
Relaxed
Rock from one foot to the other
Run
Sagged
Sank
Settled
Shifted
Showed off
Shuffle
Skidded
Skipped
Slid
Spread
Steadied
Step
Stomp
Stretch
Sunk
Supported
Swing
Tap
Tensed
Thread
Tingled
Tiptoe
Trembled
Tuck
Walk
Weakened
Wobble
Wrapped

(Description)

Bare
Big
Bowed legged
Bulging thighs
Calloused

Clumsy	Slim
Flat feet	Small
Lean	Smooth
Lissome	Soft
Long	Stems
Luxurious	Stinky feet
Muscled calves	Stocking clad
Muscular	Strong
Narrow	Supple
Perfect	Sure-footed
Petite	Tanned
Pigeon-toed	Taut
Powerful	Thick
Pudgy	Toned
Shapely	Twisted feet
Silky	Weak
Sinewy	Wide
Skinny	Wobbly
Slender	

From Tied With a Bow and No Place to Go

*Doyle put **both feet flat** on the floor, rested an elbow on the chair arm and leaned into it. "That was part of it. I'd make money on the deal, but you can't hold that against me. That's good management. I gave him a rate a half-percent lower than what he could get anywhere else. Don't forget, he came to me. I didn't con him."*

From You're Busting My Nuptials

*"No, Rayann. It's been over an hour. He isn't answering his phone. Daddy went to his house. His truck's gone. He's not coming." She started to pace. Her **bare feet sank** into the deep carpet, a small comfort against the ache the rest of*

her body was suffering. "What's wrong with me? My first husband joined the Marines to get away and now Ridge doesn't show up for our wedding. Am I that bad?"

In the above sample, I compare the comfort of the carpet to the ache she feels, and I used "was"…was suffering. This is just to point out a style choice. I could have dropped was and went with suffered, but the sentence didn't sound as good to me. Always remember, cut was when you can, but many times was, were, had, has, sound better.

From Laid Out and Candle Lit

*He eyed her from head **to toe**. Her black shorts hugged her just right. The white shirt, soft and billowy, unbuttoned far enough to see cleavage, floated as she moved. Her hair hung loose. She **was barefoot, her toes painted pink and each one had a daisy on it.***

In the above scene, Ridge has it bad. He notices everything about Tizzy, and by doing so, the reader gets a good visual, and a clear idea of how interested Ridge is!

HIPS

(Action)

Arch
Bounce
Buck
Bust (as in busted his butt)
Clench
Dip
Flex
Gyrate
Jerk
Jiggle
Lean
Lift
Lower
Moved
Nudge
Pound
Press
Pulsate
Pump
Quake
Reel
Relax
Shake
Shift
Shimmy
Shiver
Shudder
Stilled
Sway
Swing
Tense
Thrust
Tighten
Tingle
Tremble
Vibrate
Wiggle
Wobble

(Description)

Arse
Ample
Ass
Backside
Bare
Behind
Big
Booty
Bottom
Broad
Bum
Buns
Butt
Child-bearing
Chubby
Curvaceous
Delectable
Desirable
Enticing
Firm
Flat
Full-figured
Gluteus Maximus

Gluts

Hands on hips

Hard

Haunches

Hefty

Hippy

Hourglass

Large

Lean

Little

Luscious

Lush

Muscular

Narrow

Petite

Plump

Plus size

Posterior

Rear

Rear end

Round

Rump

Sensual

Sexy

Shapely

Slender

Small

Stout

Sturdy

Taut

Tight

Toned

Tush

Voluptuous

Well-rounded

Wide

Two Wrongs Make a Right

Hands on hips, *Raynie backed away, and scowled. "Are you kidding?"*

Tell Me a Secret

*The bottle blonde retreated with long fluid steps, the **sway of her hips** enough to tempt any man. Maggie wished her **own butt looked** that good in jeans. Shaking the notion from her head, she gave attention back to her new student.*

When you refer to the same thing more than once in a paragraph, or even close together on the same page, find another description to keep from echoing the same word. As you can see from the description list, there are a lot of other words you can use in place of hips!

You're Busting My Nuptials

*Tizzy folded her **feet under her hips**, rose to her knees and placed her hands on Ridge's shoulders.*

*Synola turned her back to the spectators, did a **butt jiggle-wiggle combination,** then bent double and peeked at the crowd from between her legs. She twirled around and began to unbutton her blouse and nodded toward Tizzy and Rayann. Tizzy got the message, swallowed hard and wished she had another shot of tequila.*

SPINE/BACK
(Action)

Ache
Arch
Bend/bent
Bowed
Curved
Heat
Hunched
Lean
Lurch

Relax
Shivered
Shook
Slump
Spasm
Straighten
Tensed
Tighten
Tingled
Twisted

(Description)

Beautiful
Broad
Bronzed
Chiseled
Contoured
Devine
Elegant
God-like
Hairy
Hard
Hunched
Lean
Muscular

Narrow
Ramrod-straight
Ruler-straight
Sculpted
Slender
Slim
Straight
Supple
Tanned
Taut
Trim
Well defined
Wide

Tell Me a Secret

*Deep in thought, she almost missed her exit. Luckily, the giant billboard caught her attention in time. Sweetwater, Texas~ Home of the World's Largest Rattlesnake Round-up. **A shiver ran up her spine** and back down again. Why anyone wanted to hunt the serpents was a mystery, but flat land, scrub trees, and large rock formations, provided the perfect environment.*

Laid Out and Candle Lit

*She stepped around him, **glided her hands across his back**, and moved her face in so close her warm breath floated across his skin.*

From Two Wrongs Make a Right

*He imagined her leaned back, sunshine reflecting off her raven hair, **bare toes running up and down Homer's spine,** while he half-closed his eyes in pure ecstasy.*

Don't want you to think this is some crazy fetish where my character rubs people's backs with her feet! Homer is a dog. A lazy one at that!

HEART

(Action)

Ached
Battled
Beat
Blossom
Bounce
Burn
Constrict
Demand
Drop
Expand
Failed
Faltered
Fluttered
Gallop
Grieve
Hammered
Hitch
Jumped
Kicked started
Kicked up a notch
Leapt
Lifted
Lost its rhythm
Loved
Lurched
Miss a beat
Murmured
Overflow
Plummet
Pounded

Pumped
Quickened
Race
Rebelled
Responded
Rocketed
Sank
Seethed
Seized
Settled
Shriveled
Shuddered
Skipped
Slammed
Sputtered
Squeezed
Stammered
Steadied
Stopped
Stumbled
Stuttered
Swelled
Swooned
Thudded
Thump
Thunder
Ticked
Tripped
Tumbled
Turned over

(Description)

Big
Bitter
Black
Broken
Cold
Dead
Evil
Good hearted
Hard
Heart of Gold
Heartfelt
Huge
Kind
Light
Loving
Pained
Prideful
Romantic
Steady
Sweet
Tender
Warm
Wicked

In the samples below I wanted to show heartache in a different way. In the first example, I could have said her heart sank, but by combining the ache with the sinking moon gives the character, and hopefully the reader, stronger emotion.

In the second one, same thing. She is suffering tremendous remorse and heartache, but the emotion has more power by putting it in her introspection.

From Two Wrongs Make a Right

*The moon sank and **her heart hitched a ride**. She stared back at the place. A chorus of crickets and frogs sang from the lake, and the now familiar squeak of the porch swing accompanied the melody. She took it all in wanting to remember everything. Every sound. Every moment.*

*Lying wasn't in her nature and she must have been crazy to think she could do it without guilt and shame. That combination, she'd discovered, was lethal. It tied her stomach into a knot, **turned her heart to stone**, and blackened her soul.*

Here's a heart simile. From Tell Me a Secret

*When he leaned forward and rested his arms on the table, her **heart slammed against her ribs as if a prisoner attempting a jailbreak.***

You're Busting My Nuptials

*She shoved the fear to the **deepest part of her heart**. The same place she'd kept the grief and anger when Boone died. She knew from experience, if you kept it down long enough, eventually it would go away.*

Tied With a Bow and No Place to Go

*She frowned. "He could have been here for a rendezvous and **suffered a heart attack.**"*

VOICE

(Action)

Added steel
Barked
Bellowed
Bleated
Blustered
Boomed
Brayed
Cackled
Carried
Cawed
Chattered
Chimed in
Chirped
Chortled
Clamored
Climbed
Clucked
Cooed
Cracked
Cried
Croaked
Crooned
Crowed
Diminished
Dripped
Droned
Echoed
Elevated

Gasped
Growled
Hollered
Hooted
Howl
Pierce
Pierced
Prattle
Raged
Raised
Raised an octave
Rapped
Rasped
Roared
Rumbled
Scream
Screech
Shook
Shrieked
Soared
Sob
Squeaked
Stuttered
Trailed off
Trembled
Trumpeted
Twanged
Twittered
Whimper

(Description)

Articulate
Booming
Captive
Cold
Comforting
Consoling
Cynical
Deep
Distant
Enticing
Excited
Faraway
Flat
Frosty
Full of venom
Heavenly
Hoarse
Husky
Hysterical
Icy
Kind
Loud
Loving
Low
Meek
Mellow
Muffled
Musical
Nasal
Pleasant
Primal
Quiet
Rambunctious
Raspy
Scratchy
Seductive
Sensual
Sexy
Smoky
Shifty
Shrill
Silky
Smooth
Soft
Soothing
Stage-voice
Sweet
Tender
Trembling
Unfeeling
Velvet
Warm
Weak
Weary
Whiney

You're Busting My Nuptials

*Eldora's **voice swelled and changed** to a tune Tizzy didn't recognize. The old woman became rigid, her hand tightened around Tizzy's, pinching off the flow of blood. She rocked back and forth, her hum getting louder, her movements more pronounced until she screamed out a series of jumbled words.*

ACCESSORIZE

(Action)
Buckle a belt
Cinch a belt
Hike a purse over shoulder
Kick off shoes
Knot a tie
Peel off pantyhose
Pull down a hat or cap
Release a button
Shimmy out of panties
Shrug into a coat
Shuck your boots
Sling a purse over shoulder
Slip into shoes
Slip on rings
Step into pants
Strip off pants
Thread legs or arms through pants or shirt
Tie a scarf
Toe out of boots
Tug on a vest
Unhook bra
Wrap a scarf

(Description)
Baggy
Bohemian
Casual
Comfortable
Couture
Crisp
Dated
Dingy
Dirty
Drab
Faded
Fancy
Fashionable
Filthy
Flashy
Form fitting
Formal
Frayed

Frumpy
Hand painted
Hippy
Loose
Out of style
Painted on
Pleated
Prim
Proper
Sensible
Sexy
Skinny
Smart
Stylish
Tie-dyed
Well-worn

You can't write a story without giving some fashion details. In real life, people notice what others wear, especially women. Go back to the overwriting rule and try not to describe every single thing your character has on, but give enough to help the reader get a vivid picture.

In the next example, you'll see physical description as well as fashion. Since there are two boys introduced for the first time, the reader needs that information. Try to find ways to describe characters other than stating physical facts...height, weight, hair color, etc. It also helps if you add some introspection from your POV character as to conclusions she/he draws on a first meeting. In real life, people do that. They take in first impressions, so since the reader is only privy to the POV character's assessment, try to make it interesting.

From You're Busting My Nuptials

*Tizzy approached the boys and offered her best smile and thought about produce. Denny, **a string bean of a kid, had a mop of strawberry blonde hair tussled above eyes the color of blueberries. Not gray, but not exactly blue either.** She decided they would break a lot of hearts someday.*

*Lance, **short and pudgy with a goofy smile,** paled in comparison. **A sprinkle of freckles tracked across his nose like a trail of ants on their way to a picnic.** He would definitely jump off a cliff if everyone else did.*

"Lance? I'm Tizzy Donovan. May I talk to you boys a minute?"

*Tizzy smoothed her hands over her **black turtle neck sweater.** One of her favorites, it clung to her body and covered the waist of her **skinny leg jeans,** which were neatly tucked into **leather knee boots.** The wind blew a strand of her hair across her face and she pushed it behind her ear. When Lance's eyes drifted from her mouth, to her boobs, she crossed her arms over her chest.*

By this point in the chapter, the reader knows the ages of the two boys. They are young enough to be aware of and curious about a woman's body, so a more detailed description of Tizzy's clothes is important.

Using **metaphors** to describe Denny and a **simile** to help describe Lance, keeps them from sounding alike.

In closing, please know there are plenty of successful, best-selling authors who don't follow writing rules, which proves, *rules are made to be broken.* So if you're successful with passive voice, repeat words, overwriting, etc., continue with that. Hey, *if it ain't broke, don't fix it.* However, if you have published books that aren't getting reviews or sales, you might want to take a look at the areas I've touched on here.

Listed in my recommended reading section is *Story & Style,* (June release date) by Caryl McAdoo. I highly endorse her book. She goes into detail on the problem areas I've mentioned, plus many more with tons of examples.

Dear Reader,

If you found *BODY LANGUAGE* a useful reference, I'd love to hear from you. Honest reviews on Amazon and Goodreads are always appreciated. If you would like to explore my novels, full of Southern Sass and Texas Twang, please visit: **http://www.amazon.com/s/ref=nb_sb_noss_1?url=search-alias%3Dstripbooks&field-keywords=ann+everett**

AND, if you'd like to be notified when I have promotions or new releases, please email me so that I may add you to my email list. I promise never to share your information with anyone, and only email you when I have pertinent news to share. **ann.everett@rocketmail.com**

Or, if you just have a question or comment, I always love hearing from readers.

Best Regards,

~~Ann

RECOMMENDED READING

*The Emotion Thesaurus (*Angela Ackerman & Becca Puglisi)

The 38 Most Common Fiction Writing Mistakes (Jack M. Bickham)

Story & Style (Caryl McAdoo)

ANN EVERETT BOOKS

Romantic Suspense/Mystery Trilogy

Book One—Laid Out and Candle Lit

Book Two—You're Busting My Nuptials

Book Three—Tied With a Bow and No Place to Go

New Adult/Contemporary Romance

Tell Me a Secret

Two Wrongs Make a Right

Writer's Reference

Strong Verbs Strong Voice

70542884R00058

Made in the USA
San Bernardino, CA
03 March 2018